W9-AVP-075

Our Earth

Weather and Seasons

Jen Green

PowerKiDS
press.

New York

Published in 2008 by The Rosen Publishing Group, Inc.
29 East 21st Street, New York, NY 10010

Copyright © 2008 Wayland/The Rosen Publishing Group, Inc.

First Edition

Picture credits:
Cover Dreamstime.com/Brian Grant, 1 and 12 Dreamstime.com/Jerry Horn,
4 Dreamstime.com, 5 Dreamstime.com/Martine Oger, 6 Dreamstime.com/Andre Klopper, 7 Dreamstime.com/Ernest Prim, 8 Dreamstime.com/Cora Reed,
9 Dreamstime.com, 10 Alamy/David Young-Wolff, 11 Dreamstime.com/Rene Waerts, 13 Dreamstime.com/Brian Grant, 14 Alamy/Zute Lightfoot, 15 Alamy/F. Jack Jackson, 16 Dreamstime.com, 17 Digital Vision, 18 Alamy/nagelestock.com, 19 Dreamstime.com/Bernard Breton, 20 NASA, 21 AP Photo/Weather Underground

Produced by Tall Tree Ltd.
Editor: Jon Richards
Designer: Ben Ruocco
Consultant: John Williams

Library of Congress Cataloging-in-Publication Data

Green, Jen.
  Weather and seasons / Jen Green. — 1st ed.
     p. cm. — (Our Earth)
  Includes index.
  ISBN-13: 978-1-4042-4272-2 (library binding)
  1. Weather—Juvenile literature. 2. Seasons—Juvenile literature. I. Title.
  QC981.3.G744 2008
  551.6—dc22
                        2007032602

Manufactured in China

Contents

What is weather?

Weather is what happens to the air outside. The air may be hot or cold. This can give us sunny, windy, cloudy, or rainy weather. Weather can change as clouds cover a blue sky or the Sun shines.

On the beach, we wear clothes that keep us cool. Sunscreen protects us from the Sun's rays.

⏶ Playing in the snow is fun if you are wearing the right clothes to keep you warm.

Weather is important in our daily lives. It affects the clothes we wear, how we travel around, the food we eat, and how we live.

Blowing winds

Wind is the movement of air. The Sun's heat makes the air move. When warm air heated by the Sun rises, cold air moves in to take its place. This movement of air is wind. Winds bring changes in the weather.

⌄ Kites fly best on breezy days when the wind keeps them in the air.

 **Hurricanes** are powerful **storms** with winds that can blow down buildings and cause lots of damage.

Winds may be light or strong. A light breeze moves the leaves on the branch of a tree. A strong wind tosses whole branches. A very strong wind can blow down a tree or rip tiles off of a roof.

Cloudy days

When the Sun heats the ocean, water rises as a gas called water vapor. High in the sky where the air is cold, the gas turns back to drops of water to make clouds.

❯❯ The water and ice gather to make clouds.

▲ Dark **thunderclouds** are very tall and gray.

Clouds come in many shapes. Cumulus clouds look like cotton balls and occur in fair weather. Stratus clouds spread across the sky in a gray blanket, or they can cover the ground in a fog if they are very low.

Fact

Storm clouds can gather 5.6 miles (9 km) above the ground.

Rain and snow

The tiny drops of water that make up clouds are blown around by the wind. They bump together and join to make bigger drops. The drops become heavy and fall as rain.

We use umbrellas in the rain. They are **waterproof**.

▲ Snow covers the ground until the temperature warms up and the snow melts.

Fact

In Cherrapunji, India, 30.5 ft. (9.3 m) of rain fell in one month during the **monsoon** of 1861.

In very cold air, the water in clouds turns to ice. Ice crystals join to make snowflakes. When the weather is cold, the snow falls and covers the ground.

Storms

Thunderstorms can happen in the summer. Inside the dark thunderclouds, water droplets and ice crystals rub together. The rubbing produces **electricity**.

Light travels faster than sound, so you see the lightning before you hear the thunder.

The electricity is released as a streak of lightning. The massive spark heats the air so quickly that it explodes. You hear this explosion as a loud crash of thunder.

⬇ **Tornadoes** are storms with funnels of spinning air. Inside these funnels are powerful winds that suck up objects as the tornadoes move.

World weather

Climate is the type of weather a place has over a long period of time. Different parts of the world have different climates. The part of the Earth around the equator is called the **tropics.**

Places in the tropics are hot because the Sun beats down directly from above.

Fact

The coldest temperature was recorded at Vostok, Antarctica, and was -128.6°F (-89.2°C).

◀ Snow and ice cover the polar regions for all or most of the year.

At the **poles**, the Sun is always low in the sky so its rays are weaker. These places are always cold. **Temperate** regions lie between the tropics and the poles. They have a mild climate that is neither too hot nor too cold.

The seasons

Weather changes throughout the year. These changes are called the **seasons**. Many areas have four seasons. These are spring, summer, fall, and winter.

⊻ Most animals have their young in springtime, as the weather starts to get warmer.

❯❯ In the fall, leaves turn red and orange before they fall to the ground.

Fact

Some animals eat lots of food in the fall and then sleep through the winter. This is called **hibernation**.

Winter is the coldest season. In springtime, leaves start to appear on trees and the days get longer. Summer is the warmest season. In the fall, the days get shorter and the weather starts to get colder.

What causes the seasons?

The seasons happen because the Earth tilts as it spins and moves around the Sun. During the summer, the part of the Earth where you live leans toward the Sun. In the winter, your part of the Earth leans away from the Sun.

In springtime, plants start to grow. After the summer, the weather gets cooler and many plants die or lose their leaves before the cold of winter.

The seasons affect many animals and birds. Some birds and animals travel to warmer areas for the winter. This is called **migration**.

Polar animals, such as penguins, have thick feathers or fur to keep them warm in the cold climate.

Tomorrow's weather

What will the weather be like tomorrow? **Weather forecasts** help us to see any changes in the weather. Many people rely on weather forecasts for their work.

This picture taken from space shows a spinning hurricane.

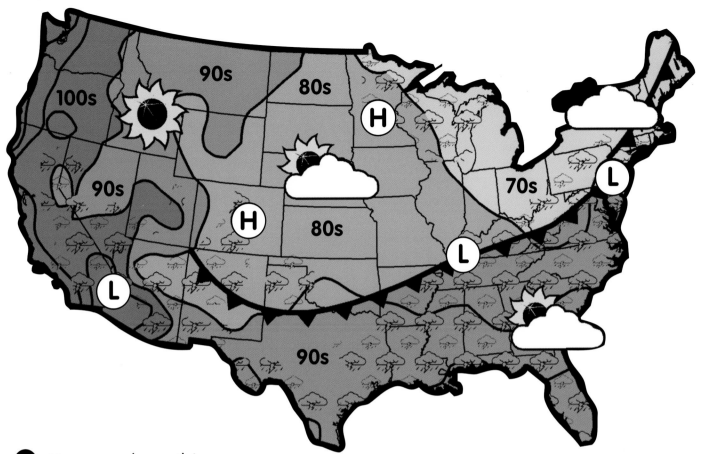

◆ Maps such as this one show tomorrow's weather. Can you see the signs for clouds and sunshine?

Experts gather information from **weather stations**. The information is fed into computers, which help to produce maps and weather forecasts.

Fact

There are over 50,000 weather stations around the world, some are even in space.

Activities

Make waves in a bowl

Waves are made by wind blowing over the sea. Make your own waves and record the results.

WHAT YOU NEED

- **Bowl with a broad rim**
- **Jug of water**
- **Paper**
- **Pencil**

1. Fill the bowl with water and put it near the edge of a table.

2. Sit down so that you can bring your mouth close to the bowl.

3. Blow gently across the bowl. Look at the wave patterns on the water's surface. Sketch the wave patterns.

4. Blow harder and draw the patterns again. Compare the two patterns.

Sketch the patterns you see in the water.

Making a weather vane

Make your own **weather vane** to find out which way the wind is blowing.

WHAT YOU NEED

- **Two pieces of card cut into triangles of different sizes**
- **Pair of scissors**
- **Two plastic straws**
- **Tape**
- **Modeling clay**
- **Empty thread spool**

5 in. (12 cm)

4 in. (10 cm)

5 in. (12 cm)

1.5 in. (4 cm)

1.5 in. (4 cm)

1.5 in. (4 cm)

1. Tape the small triangle to one end of a straw and the large triangle to the other end of the same straw.

2. Use the modeling clay to attach the other straw to the middle of the first straw, and push this through the spool. On a breezy day, hold your weather vane and watch it point to where the wind is coming from.

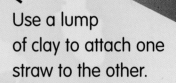

Use tape to hold cards in place.

Use a lump of clay to attach one straw to the other.

Glossary

Climate The weather a place has over time.

Electricity A type of energy that makes lightning.

Equator An imaginary line around the Earth.

Hibernation Sleeping through the winter.

Hurricanes Enormous, spinning storms.

Migration The movement of animals.

Monsoon The rainy season in the tropics.

Poles The points at the top and bottom of the Earth.

Season A part of the year that has its own weather.

Storms Bad weather with lots of rain, snow, or wind.

Temperate Between the Equator and the poles.

Thunderclouds Tall, dark clouds that create storms.

Thunderstorms Storms that produce thunder.

Tornado A funnel of air with strong winds.

Tropics The region around the Equator.

Waterproof Does not let water through.

Weather forecasts These show what the weather will be like in the future.

Weather stations Where information about the weather is collected and recorded.

Weather vane Shows where the wind blows from.

Index

Web Sites

Due to the changing nature of Internet links, PowerKids Press has developed an online list of Web sites related to the subject of this book. This site is regularly updated. Please use this link to access this list:

www.powerkidslinks.com/earth/weather